Let Real Estate Work For You As It's Doing for Me

by

Sandra Pearsall

authorHOUSE™

1663 LIBERTY DRIVE, SUITE 200
BLOOMINGTON, INDIANA 47403
(800) 839-8640
WWW.AUTHORHOUSE.COM

First published by AuthorHouse 10/04/05

ISBN: 1-4208-7943-X (sc)

Printed in the United States of America
Bloomington, Indiana

This book is printed on acid-free paper.

Dear Friends,

This is a special thanks to all of you who has supported me with my book. Many of you were a big part of my motivation to finish writing the book. You mean so much to me. I think reaching out to people with the information and motivation is the best thing I've done yet. I hope you enjoy the information I share and use it to your advantage. Thank you again and good luck.

Sandra Pearsall

Table of Contents

Introduction

Let Real Estate Work For You As It's Doing For Me

The Information in this book will help encourage you to get started investing in real estate. It will provide information as to why you should buy instead of renting. My Hope is that after reading this book you will be able to make better decisions with regards to managing your money.

Congratulations on your new beginning.

Sandra Pearsall/Author
2004

Let Real Estate Work For You As It's Doing For Me

My name is Sandra Pearsall. At 33 years of age I'm a successful real estate investor. The information I'm going to be sharing with you in this book is very important. However, before I start I want to give you some personal information about myself. I was born and raised in the City of Baltimore. I am not from a wealthy, but from a very poor family. I attended Baltimore public schools.

I come from a broken home. My parents split up when I was around 9 years old. There were 8 kids, including myself living in my household. Many times we did not know where the next meal would come from. I remember times we had no water or electricity, and sometimes we did not even have a roof over our heads. We were on public assistance, like most of the people in our neighborhood.

This is the reason I wanted to make a difference in my life. I did not graduate from high school. By age 16 I was working a minimum wage full-time job. At the time minimum wage was $3.35 per hour! I knew I could not live off that kind of income. I worked 50 hours per week and would still bring home less than $600.00 per month. I knew that I was getting nowhere fast. I later went back to school to obtain my high school diploma. I took some college courses to increase my chances of getting a better paying job. Still it lead me back to living paycheck to paycheck. Real Estate has changed my life in so many wonderful ways. I strongly believe if you want to make some extra money in your spare time or if you want financial freedom, investing in real estate is the key.

My reasons for giving you personal information about my background is so that you can see that if I can do it, anyone can.

During the years of 2000-2002, I started my own cleaning service along with working a full-time job. This was REALLY a dead end. I could not keep up with the business. It took so much out of me! My customers were mostly private residents. The cleaning was done on the weekends since I could not afford to hire a staff so, I had to do the cleaning myself. This took lots of time away from my family and from my personal life

Hours and hours of research and the experiences of others experience guided me into real estate investing. Many investors like myself invest in real estate for a number of reasons. For one, real estate is a fairly safe investment. It really doesn't matter what is going on in the stock market, people will always need a place to live.

Buy Not Rent

There is a list long of self-made millionaires who have built their wealth using real estate. Real Estate is a business where you can use other people's money to build wealth for yourself. You can use money from the banks to buy properties that you can rent or sell.

Jumping straight to the point. If I cannot encourage you to become a real estate investor, at least buy a home for yourself to live in. There are multiple benefits to owning your own home. You may get a tax reduction, potential borrowing power, and the opportunity to build wealth for yourself.

First, let me address renting. By renting you are basically building wealth for your landlord. If you rent for 15 years at the end of that 15 years you own nothing. You could pay a house off in full in that amount of time! Example: If you rent an apartment for $500.00 per month for one year. You have wasted $6,000.00. Rent normally goes up every year. When buying, your mortgage payment will stay the same. Say you rent that same house above with no rent increase for 10 years you have wasted $60,000.00. I could go on and on with examples. When you purchase a home you also feel the pride of ownership.

When looking for properties you want to find properties that are listed below market price. This way the property will have instant equity. Equity is very important. The definition of equity is the interest or value that an owner has in a property over and above any mortgage indebtedness.

Example: If you purchase a home for $50,000 but the appraised values is $75,000. You have instant equity of $25,000. This means several things. You could sell that house you bought for $50,000 for $75,000 and walk away with $25,000 profit. Or take out a 2nd mortgage or equity line of credit from the bank. You could invest the 2nd mortgage or credit line into purchasing another property or perhaps you might want to do some upgrades to the house to increase the property's value.

There are many types of properties that you can purchase with instant equity. There are Bank foreclosures, HUD, VA, and motivated sellers, etc. A lot of investors purchase to sell and make a quick profit. Many investors buy properties to rent them out for the positive income.

Money-Making Machines

Owning real estate can change your life in a very positive way. My property, shown below is a real moneymaking machine.

The property above I purchased in February of 2002. This was a HUD house. The purchase price was $15,000. The monthly payments are $117.00

per month. I rent it for $550.00 per month. I make about $430 a month profit on this one property.

Keep in mind the tenant is basically buying the house for me. This property as well as all my other properties has never had a vacancy.

People are literally lined up to rent these properties. No matter how much you talk to people about the benefit of owning they always can come up with many reason why they are not ready to buy a house. I met an investor recently who has had a long-term tenant of 20 years in one of his properties. He also owns multiple properties in Baltimore. Many of his tenants are long-term tenants.

Don't get caught up in the negative what ifs. What if I have a repair to do? What if the tenants don't pay? What if this and what if that? The "What ifs" will hold you back every time.

Use these moneymaking machines (owning real estate) to make a difference in your life. People say money doesn't make you happy.

Well it sure doesn't make you sad!!

Negative Energy

Purchased Sept 2003 Mortgage $350.00 per month. Rent for $700.00 per month, a positive cash flow of $350.00 per month

My main goal is to put this information out there for people who are really and seriously ready to make a change in their financial status. People who are tired of living paycheck to paycheck. Or people who just want to make extra money in their spare time. One thing I would like to add is information is worthless if you are not going to use it. Use it!

When I first started everyone would tell me you are taking a big risk. What if things don't work out? What if people are calling you in the middle of the night to repair things? What if you can't find good tenants? I KNEW that I was taking a risk. I'll tell you though, I would much rather risk making money rather than risk being broke. There were many negative comments made regarding my ideas about becoming a real estate investor. Most of the negative comments were from people who know absolutely nothing about real estate or who don't own anything. I did not let those people discourage me. I used their negative energy to motivate me even more.

You will need to set realistic goals to help you achieve your success. I have a goal of purchasing one to two properties a year for the next 5 years. This works for me. I'm not saying your goal must be the same.

It is whatever works for you that is most important!!!

Looking for The Right Property

My experience when looking for the right property is to try and find a property that doesn't need much work. The less money you have to put out up front means more money in your pocket. There are people out there with the skills to do remodeling. They may be a handy man or woman with experience in roofing and plumbing. People with those kinds of skills may buy a house that needs a bit more work. If they can do that kind of work themselves then great.

They may be able to get properties even cheaper than you or I. However, for the average person with no "handy person" skills may not want to search for properties that will cost a lot to get up and running.

I love renting my properties.

For the most part I can have a property ready for rent before the 1st mortgage payment is due. Usually I can do it in 2 weeks or more but certainly less than a month. All it takes is a few hours of painting of a regular town home which can be done in over the course of one or two days. Carpeting can be installed in just a few hours. Just those small upgrades can make a property look nice. I will also make sure that the grass is cut in the front yard.

Do these things and you will have people lined up to rent your home!

I purchased this property in July of 2004. The sellers paid me $5,000 at closing. The mortgage payment is $390.00 per month. The rent is $750.00 per month for a profit of $360.00 per month.

Getting Started

Many of my readers are now at the point of asking, "How can I get started?" What are the first steps? You may be excited but you may still have that fear of, "Can it really be done?"

Well, I'm going to walk you through the process from the beginning to the end.

First, you need to know that you can do it too. Anyone can. With the right information and enough motivation you can do it. There are risk in everything in life. You may have a great job where you have worked for many years and one day you could be told that you are no longer needed. Businesses are down sizing everyday. I'm for sure you know or have worked with someone who came to work one day and was fired for one reason or another. I feel that depending on a full time job is a higher risk than investing into the real estate. Like I said earlier, there are many self made millionaires who have made their millions from real estate investing. You can go into any bookstore and read about it.

Once you know in your heart that you can do it, it's time to find a lender. You will need to get pre-approved for a loan amount that will cover the price of the property you want to purchase. The key is to buy low, sell high. The property you should be interested in should be below market price. This way if you decide you don't want to rent it you can sell it and make a tidy profit. There are many mortgage companies, banks, and property owners that will finance a property to you. If your credit is really bad and you are having problems getting pre-approved you can still purchase properties using seller financing. Seller Financing is a really good way to buy real estate. All that you do is basically have the seller finance the property to you. You don't have to worry about whether or not the bank will approve you for the loan. With Seller Financing you sometimes have no closing fees and no credit check. You don't even have to show proof of income sometimes!

When you are pre-approved for the loan you can start looking for the right property. When I say the right property I mean a property that you feel comfortable with. The repairs are at the minimum and a numbers work. That is really all we are looking for. As long as it's decent, safe for living, requires little or no money and you can get it ready for rent or sell, it's the right property.

While you are on your search you will want to build a database for your business. Contractors or just general helpers should be a part of your database.

You know you may need help with painting. You can pay a few teenagers to help paint.

For helping with your property search you may want a Realtor. They can help you find properties in your price range. Don't get just any realtor. You will want someone who has experience in the business, a person who has knowledge of investment properties and knows what investors are looking for.

You will want to have a plumber who can fix things if needed.

You should also get a banker on your team who knows what you are doing and who can help you get the funds that you need.

Add an insurance agent to your team. Your property will need to be insured prior to settlement, if you are using the bank to finance.

Like any business you have to invest time into it. My experience is with real estate, if you have the right team, you may only need to invest about 5 to 8 hours a week, if not less. While I'm at work I have real estate agents looking for houses for me. If he/she runs across something that they may think I may be interested in they will contact me.

Also, I check the HUD website (www.hud.gov) on almost a daily base. I'll spend maybe 15 to 20 minutes just skimming to see if anything catches my eye.

Finally, I'm always looking and keeping my eyes open when I'm just driving around.

This property was found one morning while we were out driving looking around for another house that was for sale. Just drive around and check out other neighborhoods.

Positive Cash Flow Properties

Positive Cash Flow: is cash you receive from your property after all expenses are paid, (mortgage, taxes, insurance, etc.).

Cash Flow properties are everywhere. They are located in every state. Most cash flow properties will be found in the low to moderate-income areas. These are the areas where you will find that your working class people live. They are our teachers, plumbers, office assistants, painters, etc. These people, like myself make up 87% of the population who earn less than six figures.

Cash flow properties normally have instant equity. I purchased a 3-bedroom 1-bath townhouse for $30,000. It appraised for $60,000 at the time of purchase. That's an instant equity of $30,000.

A cash flow property can bring you steady daily, weekly, or monthly income. If your monthly mortgage and expenses on a property are $300.00 per month and you rent it for $700.00 per month you will have a positive cash flow of $400.00 per month. Is this possible? Yes it is. If you purchase the property below the marker price but now you rent it for the market price.

This is how you make it possible.

Rental Property

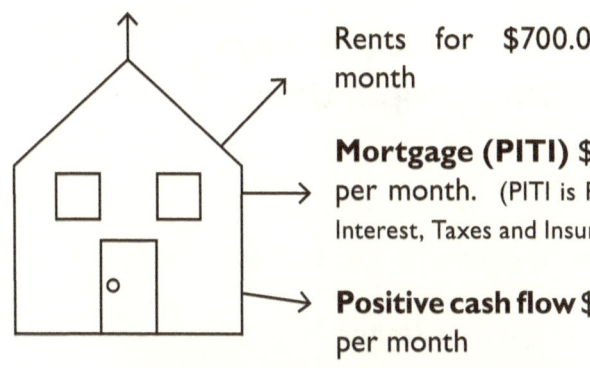

Rents for $700.00 per month

Mortgage (PITI) $300.00 per month. (PITI is Principal, Interest, Taxes and Insurance)

Positive cash flow $400.00 per month

Locating Properties

There are multiple ways of locating properties:

1. Newspaper

2. Searching the web (multiple listings)

3. Working with a Realtor

4. Checking the Bank's REO's (REOs are Bank Owned Properties)

5. Networking with other investors

6. Just driving around (For Sale By Owner)

7. For Rent Sings (Part of the hidden market)

8. Make your own sign to post in the neighborhood
    – We buy houses!
    (People will come to you)

Goals

• **Setting goals is very important. Goals give you a direction to move towards. Without goals you have nothing to strive for.**

*Write down 10 goals you want to achieve. Make sure your goals are realistic.

(Purchasing 30 properties in 20 days is not a realistic goal)

*Sign and date your goals and put it in a safe place. You will revisit them in 1 year to see where you are.

Distressed Properties

We are looking for distressed properties. IT may have an overgrown lawn, trash in yard, or be vacant. Some may only need a little paint and floor tile.

Below are some before and after pictures of my second property.

See how few dollars can make a big difference in the appearance of a property. I paid around $100.00 for paint supplies and $40.00 for the carpet for the stairs.

If you buy a property that requires rehab you will pay more.

Pictures

Before

After

After

Pictures

Before

After

Pictures

Before

After

Getting Organized

I was featured in Black Enterprise magazine for my letter on Financial Freedom in the November 2004 issue.

I received thousands of responses to the article. Many people who responded asked me the same questions. They wanted to know how I was able to purchase 5 properties in just a little over 2 years? How could they do the same? Where did I find time in my life to start investing in real estate?

The answer is I got organized.

What I have realized you cannot complete any task whether it is large or small if you are not organized. I made the decision that I was tired of just working so hard and not being able to see a dime of my money. I was paying the bill collector everything I earned.

Just by organizing your schedule so that you can fit in approximately 5 to 10 hours per week for your real estate business will pay off in a big way. It is really simple. Instead of spending 30 minutes in the morning trying to figure out what to wear arrange your clothes the night before. This will save you valuable time in the morning. You can view a few properties online in the same amount of time it takes for you to search through your closet in the morning. It takes 30 minutes or less to do a quick walk through or inspection of a property.

Organizing and using your time wisely will play a huge role in your success in real estate investing. Just take 30 minutes away from watching television and create a list of houses you would like to see. There are many ways to save time.

You must always keep a notepad and something to write with in your car. When driving around you will see a lot of homes for sale. Homes listed with a realtor, for sale by owner, HUD, VA and homes that are just empty. Many "For Sale by Owner" properties may not be listed in the newspaper. You will need to take down the phone number, address, or any other information that you may find so that you can get in touch with the seller to view and possibly make an offer. If you don't have something to take down the information on you may lose out on a good deal.

When you are ready to go out to view properties, which are for sale I suggest that you make a list of properties in the same general area. You will be able to view many more properties in the same day as opposed to driving 30 to 40 miles between properties in different areas.

Credit and Your Credit Score

Finding out your credit score will determine where you are and where to start in terms of purchasing properties. If you have good credit you can start right away by using the bank's money to buy property. If your credit is not so good, you may want to look into seller financing or assumable mortgages. Just because your credit is not so good don't let that hold you back. I will talk about seller financing and assumable mortgages a bit later in the book.

Understanding Your Credit

Credit Score range:

A- credit score range is 670-850
B- credit score range is 620-669
C- credit score range is 580-619
D- credit score range is 579-below

The banks prefer your credit score to be in the A B range in order to give you a mortgage. There are some banks that **will** approve a C range. The rates may be a little higher, but that's OK, as long as you get the financing that you need.

Understanding The Numbers

35% of your score is payment history
30% of your score is amount owed
15% of your score is length of credit
10% of your score is new credit
10% of your score is type of credit in use.

Motivation

This is a topic that I believe is going to play a large part of your real estate success. Having the know-how alone will not be sufficient if you are not properly motivated. On the other hand, some people are very motivated but do not possess the know-how. Having the right level of motivation and obtaining the proper know-how work together no matter what you do, even if it is real estate or some other endeavor.

Proper motivation along with positive thinking. You must believe that you can do it and really believe it. You will have to get rid of all the negative thinking that you have in your life. I was once told we are what we think about. If you are a negative thinker you will always have a negative outcome. Positive thinkers normally have positive outcomes. You want to be around positive people. This may mean having to change some of your friends that you spend most of your time with. Friends and family who are negative about your ideas may impact your ability to be successful.

Your life will change just from you believing in yourself. I have several motivational tools I use. My fiancée believes that I can be President of the United States. He motivates me a great deal. My godson and many of my family members keep me motivated.

There are so many people that I've met as a result of the article in Black Enterprise magazine who keep me motivated. My goal is to educate and motivate as many people as possible, all around the world.

Whatever motivates you keep it around you. Everyone must have his or her own motivational tools. It may be a dead end job, or perhaps you just hate working. It could be your past life experiences or just wanting more for your children. Whatever the reason is that motivates you post it where you can see it daily. Read it over and over again so that you are reminded everyday why you need to better your life. For me, even if I motivate my readers to buy just one house, a house to live in, then my message has made a difference in their lives.

Why rent? You are just buying a property for the landlord. Believe me, when I say, "If you can afford to rent, you can afford to buy."

Being a Landlord

Being a Landlord means that you are basically managing your own rental properties. Landlords normally market their own properties for rent. This is as simple as placing a for rent sign in the window with your phone number. You may run an ad in the newspaper.

You as a landlord have responsibilities, as do your tenants. As a landlord you should provide nice, decent and safe housing for your tenants.

This means making sure the windows and doors open and close properly. The heating and electrical should be in excellent working condition, I have chosen to paint each room in my properties so that my tenants do not have to. There should me smoke detectors on each level. I would not leave it up to the tenants to purchase smoke detectors.

A landlord is responsible for mailing out the monthly rent bills as well as collecting the rent. It really does not matter if you have your tenant mail you the rent or if you pick up the rent. As long as the rent is paid on time, I normally give the tenant a 5-day grace period to have the rent in by. If the rent is not paid by the 5th of the month they are charge the 5% late fee.

Your lease agreement determines who is responsible for repairs. I normally take on the responsibilities for the repairs if it's not a tenant related problem. Some landlord may charge a lesser rent to have the tenant responsible for repairs.

I strongly suggest you start out managing your own properties for the experience, even if you only manage them for the first year. There are property management companies that will manage your properties for you for a fee. From my research the fees can range from maybe 8% to 10% of the rent. In various counties and states the fees may be a little higher or perhaps slightly less.

When selecting a tenant no matter how great their credit background may be I always collect a security deposit. This covers most if not all of the possible damages to your property when the tenant moves out.

The tenant is responsible for making sure the rent payments are made on time.

In regards to the daily upkeep of the property the tenant is normally responsible for keeping the grass cut as well as keeping the inside and outside of the property clean.

The tenant is also responsible for any damages to the premises due to negligence or willful act.

The lease agreement is explained to the tenant before the signing of the lease. The landlord gets the original and the tenant gets a copy of the lease agreement.

A Job Vs. Investing in Real Estate

There is really no comparison to a job verses investing in real estate.

Number one you are only worth as much as you can earn with a job and are only able to afford what you can squeeze out of your paycheck. It does not matter how hard you work or how many hours you invest in the workplace. Even with yearly raises you usually cannot keep up with the cost of living. The longer you work for someone else while not investing in real estate the further behind you'll get. I'm sure you have heard the statement pay yourself first. If you are an employee the taxman gets his cute before you even see your paycheck at the end of the week.

With investing you are paying yourself first. There are so many tax breaks from owning properties. As long as you have a mortgage on the property you get to write off all the interest. the best part about it you are writing off interest that your tenant is paying. With a job you have to go to work every day even when you are sick. Not because you want to but because you know that there are about 50 people lined up to do your job.

You're basically trading time for money when you work a job and do not invest. This is the reason why many people don't spend time with their families that they should. With investing eventually you will have all the time in the world. Your investments will work hard for you. Rich people don't work hard for money. Rich people invest their money into avenues like real estate so that they don't have to work.

I'm not saying run out and quit your job. Your job is going to help you with your investing business in the beginning. What I am saying is don't plan to be poor. If you are working living paycheck to paycheck now when you retire with just a portion of that income where do you think you'll be then?

Many people feel they are stuck in their dead end jobs due to bills, bills, and more bills. This sometimes results in hostile work environments. There is a big difference when you are working because you want to work, not just because you need to be there.

I was taught all my life by my parents, family, and teachers that you have to work hard for money. For years I worked hard for my money. Now I've re-programmed my way of thinking. All that working hard for money, they can have it. I like the new way better!

Most Asked Questions and Answers

I received over 1000 e-mails from the one article in Black Enterprise magazine. Yes, I responded to them all. Many people ask the same questions. I have put together the most frequently asked questions here along with the answers to those questions. You may have had the same questions in your head.

Q: *Hello Ms. Pearsall, I read your letter to Black Enterprise about gaining financial freedom in real estate investing, I'm also in the Baltimore area and would like to start my own quest in 2005. is there any information you can offer?*

Anthony

A: Hi Anthony, Glad to hear from you. First, find out where you are with your credit. This will determine in which direction you will need to go. If your credit is good you may start right away with the bank loans. If your credit is not so good you may want to go with the seller financing.

Sandy

Q: *Hi Sandra, I had the pleasure of reading your financial freedom article in Black Enterprise magazine. Ironically, I have wanted to get into investing in rental properties.*

I live in Long Island and it's extremely expensive to buy houses. My question is how did you get started?

Everlette

A: Hi Everlette, I got started because I was tired of living paycheck to paycheck. I never had enough time to spend with my family and friends. Real estate is a sure way to buy back time. You make money while you sleep. On my first property I made $400.00 in positive cash flow. I used the equity out of my primary home to purchase my first investment property.

Sandy

Q: Sandy, My financial situation is not the best. I am only 22 years old, which makes it even harder. I already know I don't want to work for anyone for a long period of time, I just need to figure out how to get my foot in the door. Any advice would be appreciated.

Oswald

A: Hello Oswald, Get a credit check to find out where you are with your credit. Find out what you can do to improve your credit. If your credit is really bad you may want to start out with the assumable mortgage or seller financing.

To improve your credit call and close out any open credit that you are not using. You may want to look into getting a secure loan from the bank using your own money as collateral.

Sandy

Q: My name is Quincy. I am also a subscriber to Black Enterprise magazine. I was wondering if you could share with me your strategy for acquiring 5 rental properties.

Quincy

A: Hello Quincy, My main focus has been HUD, Motivated Sellers, and Bank Foreclosures. My strategy is to look for properties way below the market price so that I can make a nice profit whether I rent or sell. After I close on a good deal I'm out looking for the next one.

Sandy

Q: My name is Victoria, I really want to do it but I'm afraid. What should I do?

A: Victoria, first you have to believe that it can be done and that Victoria can do it, because you can. With the proper know-how and motivation you can do anything you put your mind to. Many people are just like you, afraid of the unknown. If you never take chance or a risk you'll never know how far you can go.

Sandy

Q: *Hello Sandra, I was reading the November issue of Black Enterprise and saw your letter. I'm from Baltimore and very interested in rental properties. I've been reading books trying to find out as much information as possible. If you have any advice...*

Brian

A: Glad to hear from you Brian. The best advice I can give you is to get started. It can make a difference in your life. Too much information without someone to guide you may discourage you from moving further. If you analyze too much you will find reasons not to do it.

Sandy

Q: *Hi Sandra, how do I locate REO's? Where do I apply for financing? Do I need a pre-approved letter? When bidding on HUD properties do you need earnest money?*

Thanks Troy

A: Hello Troy, I will try and answer all of your questions.

Number one, you can walk into any bank and request a list of their REOs. These are the properties that have been foreclose on by the bank. You can also check your mortgage companies too. A real estate agent can also get you a list of foreclosures.

Number 2, where you apply for the loan is up to you. I normally go with the bank that gives me the best rates and terms. You may also see if the bank that owns the REOs will do the financing.

Number 3, Yes, you want to submit a pre-approval letter with each offer. This shows that you are serious and can get the funds for the purchase. A seller may choose you just for that very reason.

Number 4, HUD has very strict guidelines to follow but they are in place for a good reason. You only need earnest money with HUD if your offer is accepted.

I have purchased 2 homes from HUD. Both of my experiences were very good. They even paid a portion of the closing fees.

I walked away with $6,000 Cash Back at Closing!!

Many people were shocked that I was able to walk away from closing with a $6,025.00 check in my hand. Well, I have to admit I was shocked as well. There is no science to it at all. There are no special skills needed other than just asking the seller for credits at closing. Credits are the same as cash. You determine the amount or negotiate the amount of credits with the seller. It is just that simple. The sellers will either accept your offer or not. I will include a copy of what a contract like this looks like. I made an offer on a Bank Foreclosure in July 2004 for the seller to pay me $5,000 in credits at closing along with splitting the yearly tax bill for the year. My offer was accepted. I received a check for $5,000, plus another check for $1,025.00 and the keys to my new property that I rented out very quickly. It took about $3,000 to get the property ready for rent and I still had extra cash in my pocket. It really works. I recently helped a young man with an offer on an investment property in November 2004 to receive $9,000 back at closing. The offer was accepted.

Black Enterprise Letter

In August of 2004 I wrote to the BE magazine about a great article they published called The Life of a Landlord. The article had great ideas about how to manage rental properties. My letter was published on page 24 of the November 2004 issue of Black enterprise Magazine.

Here's what I wrote…

I recently picked up the August issue of BLACK ENTERPRISE. It was absolutely the best magazine I've ever purchased. What caught my eye right away was the topic of managing the rental properties. I was able to get some great tips from this story. I'm a 33-year old black female. I started investing in real estate about two years ago, so I still consider myself a beginner. I now have five properties.
I grew up in Baltimore City in not-so-good neighborhoods. My family was very poor. I did not have an opportunity to gradate high school, but I did not let that ruin my life.
I think that every black person living in America needs to subscribe to your magazine. I've taken my opportunity. I plan to be financially free by the time that I'm, 35 years old. We all need a plan. One, who fails to plan, plans to fail.

Sandra Pearsall
Baltimore
vze3cnj4@verizon.net

As a result of this letter I've met a lot of great people who've wanted to learn how I've done what I've done. I've received thousands of emails and really enjoy helping people achieve their real estate goals and dreams.

Letters, Forms, & Process

In this section you will find letters and forms used in a real estate transaction. You will need a pre-approval letter stating that your credit has been pulled and you are pre-approved for the loan. You will want to submit a copy with each offer you make.

Once you have an offer accepted the seller will sign the contract of sale. Once you and the seller have both signed the contract, the contract is now considered ratified.

The ratified contract goes to the lender. Now the lender can start processing the loan. The lender will normally need from you, the buyer copies of recent pay stubs, W2's for the last 2 years, bank statements going back about 3 months through to the present. These items are used to process the loan.

The lender will also order an appraisal of the property. The appraisal will determine the value of the property. Most lenders are going to require a copy of the termite inspection, which the agent you are working with will handle. A termite inspection can cost around $25 to $50 dollars. You may even request that the seller pay for it. It does not hurt to ask. You will be surprised what a motivated seller will do to help you take the property off their hands.

Most sellers ask for earnest money with the contract. Earnest money can be around $100 to $1000. This money just shows that you are serious about your offer. That earnest money is still your money. Your agent will hold it with your contract until the deal is closed. Let's say you decide that you just don't want the house anymore before closing. Perhaps, you saw something else that you liked better. You could lose your earnest money for breaking the contract.

If you get an inspection and after the inspection results you decide that you no longer want the property you can normally get out of the contract without losing your earnest money. You have a licensed inspector to inspect the property for under $200.00.

It's worth getting the inspection if you have $1000 earnest money tied up in the contract.

The process will normally take 30 to 45 days.

There's normally a Title Company involved. The Title Company takes care of many things. They will take care of doing the search on the property. They also take care of registering the property with the city.

The Title Company will make sure the person selling the property has the right to sell it. The Title Company protects you. They make sure the property does not have liens on it. There are fees involved. The buyer and the seller can split the fees. Again, just ask. Keep in mind that the total closing fees normally run around $3,500. If the seller agrees to pay you at closing $6,000 or more you are not paying any of the fees. So don't let the numbers scare you. You are making "no money down" deals. Below is an example how I make my offers to get around all those fees.

My Offer:

I offer to purchase property address _____
_____ in the amount of $35,000 with the seller to give me the buyer $6,000.00 in credits at closing for repairs of my choice. Also, we will split the tax bill for the 1st year 50% /50%.

It's just that simple. Test the waters. Some sellers may accept your offer and some will not. However, the same seller that does not accept your offer today may be the same one who accepts it a month later. So, if your offer is not accepted keep the address and seller information on file.

The key is being out there making offers. Keep all emotions out of it. Keep it fun. You do not want to make offers with emotions. You may be told to make a better offer that the seller has several offers. If you wish to make a better offer you could depending on what you will get out of the deal. If it does not work for you go on to the next deal. Don't waste too much time trying to make a deal work.

The deal must work for you.

Assumable Mortgage

An assumable mortgage is basically a mortgage loan in which a buyer takes over the obligations of making the loan payments with no change in the terms of the loan.

Assumable mortgages do not have a due-on-sale clause.

The lender should be notified and agree to the assumption of the mortgage. The lender may require the buyer to qualify for the loan or may charge an assumption fee.

The seller should get in writing a release from the lender stating clearly that he / she is no longer liable for making mortgage payments. The buyer can really make out with assumable mortgages. You may acquire a property with a good amount of equity in it. The mortgage loan could have 10 years or less left on the note.

Seller Financing

Seller Financing is another way to obtain properties. With seller financing the bank is not involved at all.

This way strips away all the traditional ways of purchasing properties. The seller may ask for money down to hold the note for you. If your credit is not good this way may be perfect for you. The seller will hold the promissory note that entitles he/she to receive monthly payments from you, the buyer. There is no bank involved. You may even decide to rent that house for a positive cash flow, I've actually read that an investor should almost always ask for seller financing when making offers. The reason is that you don't have to get another credit check. Multiple credit inquires bring down your credit score. Also once you have a number of properties you are considered a higher credit risk. It may start getting harder to get loans from the bank. You don't want anything to stand in your way of your real estate business.

PRE-APPROVAL LETTER

November 6, 2004

Borrower(s):   Ms. Sandra D. Pearsall
Property:
Loan Type: CONVENTIONAL

We are pleased to inform you that the above referenced borrower is qualified to purchase a home with sales price up to $70,000. This pre-approval is based on the accuracy of the financial information obtained from the borrower, and is subject to verification. This pre-approval should not be considered a commitment to lend until all financial information, Contract of Sale, and appraisal are reviewed and deemed acceptable.

The borrower(s) credit has been pulled and is considered to be Acceptable;

any questions should be directed to the Loan Officer below.

Sincerely,

Loan Officer

_____

Forms To Use To Manage
Your Rental Properties

RENTAL / CREDIT APPLICATION

Date _____ Interviewed By _____

Name of Applicant _____ Date of Birth _____

Name of Applicant _____ Date of Birth _____

Soc Sec No _____ Phone _____

Present Address _____

City _____ State _____ Zip _____

How long have you lived at present address? _____

Name of Landlord _____ Phone _____

Prior Landlord _____ Phone _____

How many will be living in this unit? _____

Adults _____ Children _____ Pets _____

Employer _____ Occupation _____ Salary _____

How long? _____ Contact Person _____ Phone _____

Personal/Credit References

Name _____ Relationship _____ Phone _____
Name _____ Relationship _____ Phone _____
Name _____ Relationship _____ Phone _____

Applicant authorized property management to pull credit report for consideration for property leasing.

Signature _____ Date _____

SANDRA PEARSALL

Dear Applicant:

Thank you for your interest in renting from me. There will be no application fee. The security deposit is the same as the monthly rent, which is due at the time of the application. The security deposit will reserve the rental property for you while the application is being processed. The security deposit is refundable (see lease agreement). The residential lease agreement is normally 1 year. It may be renewed on a yearly basis. Rent is due on the first of each month by certified check or money order. If paid after 5pm on the 5th of the month a late charge of 5% will be due. If you have problems or questions feel free to call me at 410-000-0000. Again I want to thank you for choosing to rent from me.

Sincerely,

Sandra Pearsall

Sandra Pearsall/Owner

Renter _____ Date _____

Property Address: _____

APPLIANCES

_____ Refrigerator

_____ Stove

_____ Central Air

_____ Dishwasher

_____ Hot water heater

_____ Disposal

_____ Microwave

_____ Ceiling Fans

_____ Washer/Dryer

_____ Alarm System

_____ Furnace

|||||||||||||||||||||||||||||||||||||||||||||||||||||||||||||||||||||||||||||||||||||||

Utilities not included   X_____

**This is the monthly bill I mail
out to my tenants.**

TENANT NAME $750.00 Payment Due
                                     December 1-04

TOTAL AMOUNT   UNIT: Property Address
ENCLOSED $

                                (Money Orders Please)

SANDRA PEARSALL
P.O. Box
Annapolis Jct MD 20701

                         E-mail : VZ3CNJ@VERIZON.NET
                         Any Questions Call 000-000-0000
                                  Office 000-000-0000

SANDRA PEARSALL

Property Address _____ Date: _____

Tenants: _____

Landlord Survey

1. The Property condition: Excellent   Good   Poor

2. The neighborhood of the   Excellent   Good   Poor
   property

3. Landlord response to   Excellent   Good   Poor
   problems

4. Close to shopping area   Excellent   Good   Poor

5. Appliances in working   Excellent   Good   Poor
   condition

6. Water pressure   Excellent   Good   Poor

7. Would you rent again from   Yes   No
   the same landlord?

COMMENTS

Sandra Pearsall

(410) 000-0000

7/23/03

Dear

This letter is to inform you it's near time for the yearly inspection of the property at _____ _____. The inspection is just a walk through that should not take longer than 10 minutes. For your privacy I would like to set a date for September. You do not have to be present for this walk thru. Please call me at the number above to set a date.

We value your business.

Thank You,

Sandra Pearsall

10/1/04

To: Water Company

Customer Services from your company instructed me to send/fax a letter concerning the water bill. I am the owner of the property of _____ _____ Baltimore, MD.

I currently renting this home to tenant _____ _____ as of 10/1/03. Please change the billing to in care of the tenant. If more information is needed, you may contact me at 410-000-0000. If between the hours of 8:30am and 6:00p may contact me at work 443-000-0000.

Thank you,

Sandra Pearsall

LATE NOTICE

Date:

Dear _____

I have not received your rent payment for _____
_____, 2005 for property _____
_____. Your rent is past
due. This is a late notice. Please make arrangements
to pay your rent. Please include a $50.00 late fee if
paid after the 5th. Please contact me at 410-000-0000,
443-000-0000.

Thank you,

Sandra Pearsall

Foreclosure

I must tell you the story behind this one. It was a Bank Foreclosure. The bank hired a contractor to paint the entire house and to put in nice plush carpet throughout. They also finished the basement, which was unfinished at the time I first saw it. I did nothing at all. It was listed way below market price. I purchased it for $82,000. The market price is $175K to $195K. I just want to say, "the ball is in your corner". Keep the ball in your corner. When you are making your deals you and the seller win. You both get what you want in the end.

I love foreclosures (<u>Foreclosure Search</u>)!!!

I started investing in real estate in 2002. By the year 2005 I had purchased a total of 9 properties. My job had become the second income. I was now making more money from my rental properties than on my job.

I had finally did it. My rental income exceeded my bills. I was financially free at the age of 34. One year earlier than my original goal.

In July of 2005, I purchased a townhouse out of state. About 300 miles away in North Carolina. I do not advise a new beginner to do this. But this proves there are real estate deals everywhere, in every state, city, or town.

Where there are Real Estate agencies you can find a Management Company to manage your property if you do not care to manage the property yourself. Most management fees are around 8% to 10%, which is not a lot.

The only thing that is holding you back is you. And most people have the fear of failure.

When I started I had a lot of fear. But often reading about many self-made millionaires who had built their wealth using real estate. I said to myself I must do it. Once you truly believe in your heart that you can do it, you will make it happen.

Glossary

ARM – An adjustable mortgage rate. The interest rate of the mortgage changes periodically.

APR - Annual percentage rate

Appraisal - An estimate of the value of a property at a given date

Capital Gains - These are profits earned from the sale of real estate. The seller may defer taxes on the capital gain of his/her primary residence by buying a higher priced residence within 2 years.

Closing - The transferring ownership of a property fro the seller to the buyer in accordance with a sales contract.

Deed - A Written document by title to real property is transferred from one owner to another. The deed contains an accurate description of property.

Earnest money – A deposit made by the buyer of real estate towards the down payment of evidence of good faith

Equity - The value of a property beyond the amount owed.

Fee Simple - The absolute ownership of real property.

Foreclosure - Repossession of the property. The borrower has not met the terms of the mortgage.

FSBO - For Sale By Owner

Income Property - Real Estate that generates rental income

Mortgager - The Borrower

Mortgagee - The lender

PITI - Principal, Interest, Taxes, and Insurance

Real Estate - Land including the building on it

Seller Financing – The owner or seller finances the property for you instead of the bank

Title - Evidence that the owner of the property is lawful possession.

About the Author

I'm 34 years old. Born and raised in Baltimore Maryland. Had a rough start in life. My parents split up when I was around 9. This was very hard on the family.

By the time I was 19 I was married. Six years later that ended in divorce. That was a very tough period in my life but I knew that I would overcome it. I always had a dream that I was going to be somebody. Being broke is what I learned as a young child. Mama was always broke. We went without a lot. Many times Mama did not have money to feed us. Most of the people in my neighborhood had nothing but we always managed to have even less than them. If you know what I mean. Going back to the age of 16 I dropped out of high school. I was living on my own at age 17. I experienced a date rape which I ended up pregnant. I lost the baby due to a miscarriage.

Working at restaurants sometimes 2 at a time to make ends meet. I felt to quit everyday but I did not want to end up a victim of circumstances. I saved enough money to take the Nursing Assistant Training which quickly landed me a job making $5.25 per hour. This was about $2.00 more per hour than the restaurant jobs.

I worked at the Nursing Home for 4 years. I received several promotions but still made under $9.00 per hour. I was still getting no where fast. The best decision I made was to invest into real estate. With the real estate I have made up to $34,000 with one real estate transaction. That's more money than I make working 40 hours a week for a whole year. I now own multiple rental properties. I can afford to help others now. Never let obstacles hold you back. If I can do it you can too.